Julie Koerner

FRIEDMAN/FAIRFAX
PUBLISHERS

A FRIEDMAN/FAIRFAX BOOK

Library of Congress Cataloging-in Publication number available upon request.

ISBN 1-56799-541-1

Editor: Nathaniel Marunas
Art Director: Jeff Batzli
Designer: Ruth Diamond
Photography Editor: Grace How
Production Director: Karen Matsu Greenberg

Color separations by Ocean Graphics International Company Ltd.
Printed in Hong Kong by Wing King Tong Co. Ltd.
1 3 5 7 9 10 8 6 4 2

For bulk purchases and special sales, please contact:
Friedman/Fairfax Publishers
Attention: Sales Department
15 West 26th Street
New York, NY 10010
212/685-6610 FAX 212 /685-1307

Visit our website: http://www.metrobooks.com

Contents

The big band sound is an eclectic style of music produced by bands that generally have more than ten members, featuring saxophones and brass instruments, piano and drums. It reached its height of popularity during the twelve years between 1935 and 1947 and touched every major city in the United States and many in Europe. But the big band craze did not appear overnight; it was the culmination of a social and musical evolution that began almost fifty years earlier, at the dawn of the twentieth century. It had roots in West African cultures, yet assimilated European classical music; it incorporated American religious, minstrel, and folk songs; and it contributed to the development of jazz.

Popular theory connects the origins of dance band music to another favorite American pastime: baseball. In 1913, a musician and ardent baseball fan named Art Hickman followed the San Francisco Seals to their training camp in Sonoma County, California. With the approval of team manager Dell Howard, Hickman arranged a series of evening dances to relieve the tedium of the long training season. Hickman assembled an eight-piece band consisting of piano, trombone, trumpet, drums, two banjos, a violin, and a string bass. Everyone, including the reporters encamped with the baseball team, was impressed with the music, and before long, the band, which soon included two trombones, was performing at the St. Francis Hotel in the heart of San Francisco. It was during one of their frequent engagements at the St. Francis, possibly at the 1915 San Francisco World's Fair, that the band caught the attention of a New York theatrical producer named Florenz Ziegfeld. He took them to New York in 1919, where, among other venues, they played in the exciting and sometimes scandalous Ziegfeld Follies.

Irene and Vernon Castle.

The First Dance Bands

Before the early twentieth century, public dancing was not a popular or particularly acceptable pastime. But not long after the turn of the century, Vernon Castle, an English magician, and his American wife, Irene, formed an energetic dance team that invented the fox trot, the turkey trot, the bunny hop, and several other dances that sparked new activity on the dance floor. Suddenly, in the 1920s, everyone was dancing, and the popularity of dance bands spread. Bands with names such as The Scranton Sirens, The Melody Makers, The Syncopating Five,

Outdoor dining and dancing in Palm Beach, Florida.

Territory Bands

Trumpet player Cootie Williams

During the 1920s and 1930s, while big bands were thriving in places such as Chicago and Los Angeles, another kind of band music was making its mark outside of the cities. In smaller, more rural parts of the country, bands were formed by young, most often black, musicians with little means or resources and few choices about where they could play and with whom. Circuses, school or local bands, boats along the Mississippi River, and traveling minstrel shows became their venues. These bands, because they traveled in nomadic fashion within a limited area, came to be called territory bands.

Most of the territory bands that left any record behind for historical scrutiny were so far removed from mainstream musical influences that they had little exposure to jazz. Any musical education their leaders may have had was classical, and the music that evolved out of these territory bands was an eclectic mix of classical, modern, and ragtime. There were scarcely any recordings made of these bands, but the few that exist demonstrate that much of this music, although isolated, was as creative, improvisational, and sensational as that in the big cities.

One of the best territory bands was the Nat Towles Orchestra, based in Omaha, Nebraska. The few surviving records from the Towles band indicate a high caliber of talent, raising the possibility that they would have met with success in larger cities. Perhaps Nat Towles feared, probably correctly, that if he exposed his band to larger audiences he might lose his players to more famous bands (or to bands that paid higher wages).

There were several other territory bands who left behind a memorable body of work, however small. The Carolina Cotton Pickers stayed together from 1929 through 1944, and featured trumpet player Cat Anderson, who went on to play with Lionel Hampton and Duke Ellington. A short-lived ten-piece band from Miami, called Ross De Luxe Syncopators by bandleader Alonzo Ross, introduced trumpet player Cootie Williams to the world. Like the Nat Towles Orchestra, Red Perkins' Dixie Ramblers were based in Omaha. The Ramblers were distinctive because several of their band members played more than one instrument; this enabled them to create a big band sound with only a few personnel. Jimmy Gunn's Dixie Serenaders came from Charlotte, North Carolina. Los Angeles, too, spawned a few noteworthy territory bands, such as Sonny Clay's Plantation Orchestra (later called The Dixie Serenaders as well), Curtis Mosby and his Dixieland Blue Blowers, and Paul Howard, whose band later became associated with Louis Armstrong.

and Rector's Novelty Orchestra came out of Chicago, Kansas City, New Orleans, Portland, Boston, Los Angeles, Atlantic City, Denver, and other cities.

Fred Waring's Orchestra with vocalists the Lane Sisters.

"Roaring Twenties" dance music manifested itself in many ways, and was played by a colorful assortment of bands. Besides their catchy names, members of some of the more gimmicky bands wore matching striped jackets, clown outfits, or pilot attire. One thing these bands had in common was that they all had a large number of members, ranging from eight to twenty or more; otherwise, each orchestra tried to develop a personality and following of its own. Some bands played a completely popular dance repertoire, while others played more jazz-like music, venturing into a new style that came to be known as swing.

Ballroom Dancing

To attract better bands as well as larger audiences, some ballrooms initiated band competitions during which two bands played alternating sets. Each band would play a half-hour set, and the audience would cast their votes with applause. This gimmick provided exposure for some excellent bands and at the same time delivered nonstop music for the audiences. Some of the early ballrooms were the Savoy in Chicago; Roseland and Arcadia in New York; Glen Island Casino just outside New York City; the Graystone in Detroit; and Arcadia Ballrooms in Los Angeles and several other cities. Hotels such as the Coconut Grove and the Biltmore in Los Angeles; the Mark Hopkins, St. Francis, and Palace Hotels in San Francisco; and the Biltmore, Roosevelt, and Taft Hotels in New York opened classy, glamorous rooms. Chicago opened the Trianon and the Aragon ballrooms, and soon there were dance halls with the names Trianon, Aragon, and Arcadia in several cities.

The "Swing Step" quickly became popular.

Guy Lombardo in **Many Happy Returns,**
starring George Burns and Gracie Allen.

Big Bands in the 20s

The mid-1920s was also the time of
Prohibition. An amendment to the
Constitution made it illegal to make, trans-
port, or buy alcohol in the United States.
Because of the law, alcohol consumption
was significantly curtailed and drinking was
pushed underground into "speakeasies" and
private clubs. To attract customers, these
clubs booked the best bands they could,
hoping popular entertainers would bring in
large crowds that would buy plenty of liq-
uor. The better bands sometimes found
they had an extended booking in these
clubs, whether or not they wanted it. If they
drew large audiences, management often
used mob strong-arm tactics to "induce"
them to stay on indefinitely. These clubs
were often raided late at night; though
everyone in the club was arrested, only the
owners were prosecuted. But that didn't
stop jittery customers from jumping on the
bandstand at the first sign of a police raid,
pretending to belong there.

But the Depression put a damper on
exuberance of every kind, and led to the
brief emergence of the so-called "sweet"
bands of Guy Lombardo, Isham Jones, and
Hal Kemp. Romantic crooners such as Rudy
Vallee also caught on. While the sweet
bands were consistently popular, with
smooth violin sections and romantic songs
and singers, the commercial environment
was soon ripe for innovative change.

Opposite: Music by Rudy Vallee, whose syrupy
voice won him many admirers.

Glen Gray (1906–1963) and the Casa Loma Orchestra

In Detroit in the mid-thirties, the Casa Loma Orchestra was begun by Henry Biagini, Glen Gray, Peewee Hunt, and Billy Rausch. A few years later, Biagini was dropped and the remaining members plus several others formed the first "cooperative band," in which each player had an equity interest. Its manager was Francis O'Keefe, who would later form the Rockwell-O'Keefe booking office. Glen Gray and the Casa Loma Orchestra, as it came to be called, made itself attractive both aurally and visually, for they always wore tuxedos and displayed exaggerated manners onstage. Audiences loved their ability to effectively play a jazzy big band number, then move right into a sentimental ballad. They stayed together over ten years, until the middle of the forties, when big bands began to fizzle.

Two record company promotion pictures of Glen Gray.

SMOKE RINGS

Introduced by
GLEN GRAY
and his Original
CASA LOMA
ORCHESTRA

Earl Hines (1905–1983)

Earl "Fatha" Hines was an extraordinary pianist who played with Louis Armstrong in The Louis Armstrong Hot Five in 1927. When interest in big band music reached its peak, Hines already had his own band in Chicago with singers Walter Fuller and Herb Jeffries, trombonist Trummy Young, who later played with Jimmie Lunceford and Louis Armstrong, and tenor saxophonist Jimmy Mundy, who later became one of Benny Goodman's musicians and arrangers. When the boogie-woogie style of piano playing became the craze in the early 1940s, Hines fit right in. By then, his band included singer Billy Eckstine, saxophonist Charlie Parker, Dizzy Gillespie on the trumpet, and another singer named Sarah Vaughan. Their music was some of the best jazz of the era, but unfortunately, little was recorded during this time because of a musician's union recording ban. In the late forties, Hines played with Louis Armstrong, then began appearing solo through the sixties.

Paul Whiteman

Of the many bands that migrated to New York from the West Coast, Paul Whiteman's (1890–1967) was the most influential and memorable. Regarded by some as the "King of Jazz," Whiteman was revolutionary in several respects. He was the first bandleader to fully arrange his orchestrations, thus allowing audiences to become familiar with them. Whiteman was also the first to have a female vocalist (Mildred Bailey, who sings with the Benny Goodman Orchestra on "I Thought About You") and the first to have a vocal trio (Bing Crosby, Harry Barris, and Al Rinker, also known as the Rhythm Boys, sang

Above: Mr. and Mrs. Paul Whiteman sail to England on tour. Left: The Rhythm Boys, left to right, Al Rinker, Bing Crosby, Harry Barris.

with Paul Whiteman during his most popular years). Whiteman's orchestra played vaudeville first, and went to Europe before any other bands toured outside the United States.

Also, Whiteman was truly liked and respected by his musicians, undoubtedly because he treated them with respect, both personally and musically. A monumental showman, both in size and personality, with an infectious enthusiasm for exciting music, Whiteman was never reluctant to showcase

Paul Whiteman's weekly network radio broadcast featured Broadway comedian Lou Holtz.

talent, and many of his band members, such as Tommy and Jimmy Dorsey, Bix Beiderbecke, Jack and Charlie Teagarden, Joe Venuti, Bing Crosby, and Johnny Mercer, would go on to illustrious careers thanks in large part to Whiteman.

Fletcher Henderson

During the 1920s, Paul Whiteman's band, first called "The Californians" (many others would use that name too), was a dominating force in the musical world, along with the bands of Paul Specht, Jean Goldkette, Ben Pollack, and Fletcher Henderson (1898–1952). Henderson's contributions to this genre of music were monumental, but his name was less familiar in commercial music circles because he was black.

Music produced by black bands during the surge of big band popularity was exemplary, but the social conditions of the time prohibited black bands from playing in the hotels and ballrooms that promised the most commercial exposure. Fletcher Henderson, Bennie Moten, and Duke Ellington had been playing innovative forms of big band jazz for years prior to the craze for dance bands. In fact, the black musical community had already named a jazz-inspired royal hierarchy in "King" Oliver,

King Oliver (1885–1938)

One of the earliest recorded giants in jazz history is cornet player, composer, and bandleader Joe Oliver, nicknamed "King" by his peers. Coming out of New Orleans in the early 1900s, King Oliver has been called the greatest performer of New Orleans jazz. During his early years, Oliver took a boy named Louis Armstrong under his wing, nurturing and encouraging his formidable skills. Later, in Chicago, Armstrong played with Oliver's Creole Jazz Band. Oliver made some recordings with several bands, most notably King Oliver and his Dixie Syncopators, but the popularity of his style of music began to fizzle with the rise of swing. Known throughout his life as "Papa Joe" to Louis Armstrong, and King to everyone else, Oliver, blind in one eye

since childhood, died toothless and penniless. Only since his death has his substantial influence on jazz been appreciated.

"Duke" Ellington, and "Count" Basie, before the white-controlled commercial music business began handing out titles such as "King of Swing."

Fletcher Henderson, in particular, is credited with developing, arranging, and writing music in the creative, innovative style soon to be called swing. The swing style varied an arrangement by inserting syncopated sections into the regular beat, skipping octaves, or singling out instrumental sections at unpredictable times and places, changing the pace from the familiar to the unexpected. This exciting style widely expanded opportunities for musicians and singers to showcase their talents through solo parts within a number. Henderson called his music "Big Band Jazz" and his mid-twenties band featured Louis Armstrong, Coleman Hawkins, Cootie Williams, Edgar Sampson, and Fats Waller. It had a tremendous influence on many musicians, including, among others, Benny Goodman.

Duke Ellington (1899–1974)

While other bandleaders formed, disbanded, and reformed new bands, Duke Ellington remained a consistent bandleader for over fifty years. As a pianist, singer, and composer, Duke Ellington made a greater contribution to music than any other bandleader. Ellington began with a small group in 1924, and had a band with fourteen instrumentalists and a singer by 1932. Throughout the next four decades, he continued to play jazz, blues, and popular songs with larger and smaller bands until his death in 1974.

During the 1930s, while Benny Goodman, Glenn Miller, and others were enjoying their peak of success in the United States, Duke was traveling through Europe, where he was adored.

In fact, Ellington's bands never achieved the commercial success of some of the other bands in the United States. This was in part because, as a black band, they did not have access to the same commercial exposure as their white counterparts, and in part because Duke selected music according to his own, not his audience's, standards. He could, and he did, write and play popular songs, but he was frequently unwilling to compromise his musical ethics for the sake of commercial success.

Throughout the many years with his band, Ellington earned a reputation as an incomparable leader. He chose great musicians, such as Johnny Hodges, Cootie Williams, Lawrence Brown, Jimmy Blanton, Billy Strayhorn, and singers Ivy Anderson and Herb Jeffries. He gave his musicians the kind of artistic inspiration and freedom that other bandleaders might have been reluctant, or unable, to grant. Ellington was not only a peerless arranger, but a master composer as well, and his songs "Sophisticated Lady," "Caravan," and the signature song of an entire period in the development of jazz, "It Don't Mean a Thing If It Ain't Got That Swing," immortalized the Duke thoughout the entire world.

On May 25, 1974, at the age of seventy-five, Duke Ellington died of pneumonia in a hospital in New York City. With Ellington's death the jazz world lost one of its most influential and monumental figures. Ample testimony to his legendary stature had been accorded him only a couple of weeks earlier, when *Down Beat* magazine honored the occasion of his birthday with an entire issue devoted to the man and his incomparable legacy of music-making. The issue included praise from such luminaries as conductor Leonard Bernstein and trumpeter Miles Davis. Some of the most heartfelt admiration and respect was expressed by Louis Bellson, a drummer who had worked for Benny Goodman, Tommy Dorsey, and finally the Duke himself in the early 1950s: "You, the MAESTRO, have given me a beautiful education musically and have guided me to be a good human being. Your valued knowledge and friendship will be with me forever. You are the model citizen of the world. Your music is Peace, Love and Happiness."

Louis Armstrong (1900–1971)

Often singled out as the greatest solo performer of all time, Louis Armstrong mastered the art of swing with uncommon finesse and beauty. Beginning in the 1920s, playing second cornet first with King Oliver and later with Fletcher Henderson, "Satchmo" went on to play in his own smaller groups called The Hot Five and Hot Seven.

Armstrong's playing style, on cornet and trumpet, was remakably expressive and technically superior. Satchmo also had a great singing voice, and may have invented the "scat" singing he became well-known for. After some rough times and ineffective management, Satchmo hooked up with Joe Glaser, forming a successful partnership. By the 1950s, Armstrong was playing with a group called the All-Stars, whose original members included Earl Hines and Jack Teagarden. Armstrong and the band played throughout Europe. He became an American goodwill ambassador, a role he enjoyed until 1957, when he could no longer tolerate the country's prejudice against his own race. But he continued to play with his band until his death in 1971.

Bix Beiderbecke (1903–1931)

He lived for only twenty-eight years, but Bix Beiderbecke left behind a legacy that is revered by jazz enthusiasts, due in part to the drama of his tragic life and early death, and in part to his status as the first great white jazz musician. Never learning to read music (but already playing improvisational cornet learned from Original Dixieland Jazz Band records) and meeting Louis Armstrong on a riverboat are two major factors that contributed to Bix's musical foundation and to his appreciation of the revolutionary improvisational jazz played by the black bands. By the time he was twenty, Bix Beiderbecke was recording many of his own compositions with the Wolverines, and soon after he played with Paul Whiteman's band. As King Oliver was mentor to Louis Armstrong, so Armstrong was to Bix Beiderbecke: according to legend, Beiderbecke is the only person to whom Armstrong ever lent his horn in order to hear him play.

Benny Goodman

As a child, Benny Goodman (1909–1986) studied clarinet with a strict classical disciplinarian named Franz Schoepp. Goodman joined the musicians' union at thirteen and was sitting in with many different bands by his late teens. Even then, his clarinet playing ranged from disciplined perfection to impromptu invention, and the musical world started to take notice. Around 1924, he began to play with Ben Pollack, with whom he made his first recordings. During the next few years, Goodman played with various bands, including those of Ted Lewis and

Paul Whiteman, and with George Gershwin's Broadway Theatre orchestra.

In addition to working freelance on the radio, Benny Goodman became a popular studio musician and spent the first years of the 1930s recording with many different bands under the Columbia Records house band led by Ben Selvin. In this capacity, Goodman became well acquainted with many top musicians such as Gene Krupa, Charlie Teagarden, and Tommy Dorsey.

By all accounts, the commercial success and wide popularity of the big band sound began with Benny Goodman. He struggled for acceptance in the early years of his band career, forming his first unit in 1934 and playing his first engagement in July of that year at Billy Rose's Music Hall in New York. The show was a flop, but the band caught the attention of radio producer Joe Bonime, who hired Goodman and his group to participate in the broadcast of a three-hour, three-band, Saturday night music marathon. The other bandleaders were Xavier Cugat

Benny Goodman leads his orchestra during a radio concert.

Records and Radio

Before compact disc players, before stereos, even before record players, people listened to music through a large horn on their "talking machines." A spring-driven motor required careful wind-up, then played a ten-inch disc recorded on only one side. This lasted until 1905, when both Victor and Columbia made improved machines that amplified sound more effectively. By the 1920s, when bands began to be widely recorded, home listeners played their records on a wind-up phonograph with steel needles that required frequent replacing.

In 1906 The Mills Novelty Company in Chicago introduced the first jukebox, which could hold seven ten-inch discs. Soon after, commercial competition began between the Victor Company, which eventually became RCA Victor, and Columbia Records, now Sony Music Entertainment.

To record a disc in the 1920s, musicians and singers gathered around a single microphone. Sounds that were too far in the background sometimes didn't even record.But electronic advancements came rapidly and records soon had better fidelity, lifting them out of the novelty category and into the mainstream.

Record companies today rely heavily on radio to help sell their product. Few records become hits without significant airplay. But in the early days of both mediums, the opposite was true. The rise of radio broadcasting caused a downturn in record sales. Radio listeners heard only music, good or bad, without any kind of identification. Even if listeners wanted to buy the record they were hearing, they weren't told what it was. By 1928 the Federal Radio Commission instructed broadcasters

Left: The Wurlitzer jukebox, a far cry from the 1906 Mills Novelty Company version that held only seven discs.

to announce the titles of the records they played. In 1929, the Artists' Protective Society asked radio stations to pay royalties for the music they broadcast because the musicians were rapidly losing money from the decline in record sales.

During the Depression years, record companies tried to reach the college market by providing affordable, portable record players and inexpensive one-sided paper discs. The promotion was called "hit-of-the-week," and each week a new disc was released in hopes that the music-loving younger generation would buy it.

By 1934, the jukebox was greatly improved, and Columbia, Victor, and Brunswick Records were joined by a fourth competitor, Decca. Record sales and jukebox exposure created high-volume big band interest by the latter part of the 1930s. According to a 1940 *Billboard* magazine chart, the top five retail discs in July were:

1. "I'll Never Smile Again," Tommy Dorsey
2. "The Breeze and I," Jimmy Dorsey
3. "Imagination," Glenn Miller
4. "Playmates," Kay Kyser
5. "Fools Rush In," Glenn Miller

Capitol Records was formed in Hollywood in 1942 and quickly became a major player in the record business. One of its original partners was Johnny Mercer, whose intent was to make recording conditions better for the artists. Mercer was perfectly suited to the task of reorganizing the recording industry to be more sympathetic to the needs of musicians; he himself was a singer and songwriter (he had worked with the Dorsey brothers, Paul Whiteman, and Benny Goodman) and understood the importance of a healthy working relationship between musicians and recording companies.

At its start, Capitol Records made two major innovations: acknowledging the value of good relations with radio disc jockeys, and publishing a free weekly news magazine, which enabled fans to become more familiar with their favorite recording stars.

Bunny Berigan
(1909–1942)

To most people who heard or played with him, Bunny Berigan was one of the world's greatest trumpeters. As a player with Frank Cornwall, Hal Kemp, Benny Goodman, and finally Tommy Dorsey, Berigan's skill on the trumpet was outstanding. In 1937, he left Dorsey's band to form one of his own, for which he recruited arranger Ray Conniff, pianist Joe Bushkin, and drummer Buddy Rich. But his leadership qualities were not as strong as his musical talents, and he disbanded around 1940. He again joined Tommy Dorsey, though they split before the year was out. He tried to form a new band, but failing health was catching up with him and he died at age thirty-three of cirrhosis of the liver.

BUNNY BERIGAN
Plays Selmer Trumpet Exclusive

and Kel Murray. The *Let's Dance* radio program lasted twenty-six weeks. Soon after their *Let's Dance* appearance, the Goodman band was hired to follow Guy Lombardo in the Grill Room of the Roosevelt Hotel in New York—there, too, the band received a lukewarm reception.

With the persistent help of jazz enthusiast, record producer, and avid fan John Hammond, and also of MCA agent Willard Alexander, Benny Goodman's band planned a cross-country tour in 1935. The band plodded along from city to city getting only mediocre responses. In fact, in Denver, Goodman was mortified to learn that some people had demanded their money back. But the power of radio was at work as the tour progressed and big band music was beginning to impress

Lionel Hampton (b. 1909)

As a child in Wisconsin, Lionel Hampton was taught to play a snare drum by a Catholic school nun. As a teenager in Chicago, he took a job as a newsboy because the newsboy band marched in parades. He played vibraphone with Louis Armstrong, then with Benny Goodman, and later formed recording groups that included Gene Krupa, Harry James, Dizzy Gillespie, Teddy Wilson, Benny Carter, Chu Berry, Coleman Hawkins, and Ben Webster. By late 1940, he left Goodman to form his own band, which still performs after many decades of change. This band has included such greats as Ziggy Elman, Cootie Williams, Harry James, Dizzy Gillespie, Lawrence Brown, and Benny Carter. In the 1950s, the band enjoyed a resurgence of success thanks to an eighteen-year-old producer named Quincy Jones.

demanding musical standards. For instance, when Goodman was forced to take a break for back surgery in 1940, several of his band members, including vocalist Helen Forrest (whom Benny had hired in late 1939 when the Artie Shaw band broke up), waited to re-form a new band later in the year.

Because of his early formal training, Goodman enjoyed playing with classical musicians as well as with swing musicians. In December 1940 he performed as guest soloist with the New York Philharmonic at Carnegie Hall, playing the Mozart Clarinet Concerto and Debussy's First Rhapsody.

For the next few years, Goodman kept his band intact, continued to perform with symphonies, and recorded many more records. It was not unusual for the Goodman band to perform at a dinner club until late at night and then gather together with friends and fellow musicians for an improvised session that sometimes lasted until the sun came up. By the mid-forties the band had counted among its members Peggy Lee, Mel Powell, and trombonist Bill Harris, who would go on to become a famous member of the Woody Herman Band. After the popularity of big band music began to wane in the mid-forties, Benny Goodman remained a major contributor to and influence on the music world until his death in 1986.

Benny Goodman publicity photograph.

Chick Webb (1902–1939)

The Savoy Ballroom in Harlem was drummer and bandleader Chick Webb's home base for most of the thirties. The Savoy management liked to hold "contests" between bands, and one of the most famous was in 1937 between Benny Goodman's Orchestra, with Gene Krupa drumming, and Chick Webb's outfit. According to most accounts, Chick Webb's band, which played second (and was the house band) was the unanimous winner. Soon after, Webb brought singer Ella Fitzgerald to his band, and together with saxophonist and arranger Edgar Sampson, the band made history. Their success was cut short when Chick contracted tuberculosis and died in 1939. Ella acted as leader of the band for awhile, but things were not the same without Webb, and Fitzgerald eventually went out on her own.

Big Band Vocalists

Left: Charlie Barnet discoverd Lena Horne. Below: Frank Sinatra's first paying job in music was at the Rustic Cabin in Englewood, New Jersey.

There were many reasons for bands to change vocalists. Sometimes, a singer's style might be perfectly suited to one band, yet unable to blend effectively with another. Cramped traveling and working conditions made it easy for clashes between band members (and sometimes between bands) to occur. On the other hand, there were also many marriages within the bands. Woody Herman's band seemed to have more than an average share of singers who married musicians. Some vocalists, such as Ella Fitzgerald in Chick Webb's band, and Anita O'Day with Gene Krupa, helped to establish the band's style.

Many vocalists whose names are familiar today began their careers in big bands. Frank Sinatra began with Harold Arden, moved to Harry James, and then to Tommy Dorsey on his rise to fame. Peggy Lee, Doris Day, Vaughn Monroe, Helen O'Connell, Perry Como, Kay Starr, Joe Williams, Helen Forrest, Dick Haymes, Lena Horne, Rosemary Clooney, Dinah Washington, and Ginny Sims all sang for at least one orchestra, usually many more.

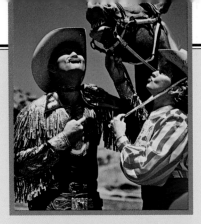

There were also many people who began their careers by singing in a band and then took a different direction altogether. Merv Griffin sang with Freddy Martin, but made his entertainment mark as a television personality, as did Mike Douglas, who once sang with Kay Kyser. Fred Waring began as a bandleader, formed a famous and long-lived glee club, remained in the music business throughout his career, and also found time to invent the Waring Blender.

Bandleader Ozzie Nelson married his singer, Harriet Hilliard, in 1935, and the two eventually became famous for their television show *Ozzie and Harriet*. The Nelson family, although plagued by more than its share of tragedies, is now in its third generation of music-makers. Dale Evans, who went on to a successful marriage and partnership with her husband Roy Rogers, once sang for Anson Weeks. Betty Grable, Dick Powell, Fred MacMurray, Jane Russell, Gene Barry, Alice Faye, Art Carney, and Betty Hutton were all singers who went on to find their careers in television and movies.

Above, left: Roy Rogers and Dale Evans were beloved television personalities. Above, right: Peggy Lee was a songwriter as well as an outstanding vocalist. Left: Kay Starr sang with Charlie Barnet and Joe Venuti.

How Big Bands Were Born

Quite frequently and quite understandably, top musicians would often leave one band to form another on their own. By the same token, almost all successful leaders had at one time been sidemen for someone else. Of course, this sort of transmigration often meant that, musically speaking, the genre was something of a melting pot. Tenor saxophonist Charlie Barnet's band showed strong influences of Duke Ellington and Coleman Hawkins. Cornet player Louis Armstrong became famous as a great soloist and bandleader. No one could stay off their feet when Jimmie Lunceford's band, known for its outstanding showmanship, began to play. Count Basie, always a musicians' favorite, had his own popular style: his arrangements began in the rhythm section, moved to tenor sax, then opened to the entire band. Basie introduced many artists to audiences early in his career, which lasted over forty-five years, and later featured the talents of vocalist Ella Fitzgerald and drummer Buddy Rich, among many other jazz luminaries. The Casa Loma Orchestra was

Billie Holiday's first recording was with Benny Goodman in 1933.

the most popular band on college campuses until the Dorsey Brothers, featuring Glenn Miller, appeared on the scene.

When the Dorsey Brothers, who were known for their frequent altercations, finally split in an onstage blow-out, Jimmy stayed with the orchestra and hired vocalist Helen O'Connell to sing with the wildly popular Bob Eberly. Tommy Dorsey, one of the all-time great trombonists, formed his own

Tommy and Jimmy Dorsey, reunited in 1953.

Jimmie Lunceford (1902–1947)

Jimmie Lunceford, a high school athletic director from Memphis, Tennessee, became one of the Big Band era's most popular bandleaders. Limited to lesser performance places because his was a black band, Lunceford turned to recording, producing some of the swing era's most popular tunes with arranger Sy Oliver.

As a performing unit, the Lunceford band was pleasing not only to the ear but to the eye; the members dressed in fancy top hats and tails, and moved in a choreographed fashion that became a forerunner for many of the popular bands of the near future. Lunceford put together a band that consisted of former athletes like himself as well as musicians with classical training, resulting in an eclectic yet disciplined style of music. Musicians Willie Smith, Trummy Young, Jimmy Crawford, Eddie Tompkins, and Joe Thomas all played with Lunceford's band. At the height of popularity of the big bands, Jimmie Lunceford was a consistent presence, giving performances that thrilled audiences everywhere. But road travel was far more strenuous at the time for black bands than for white, and in 1947 Jimmie Lunceford died of a heart attack while on the road.

Jimmie Lunceford (top) and one of his bandmembers.

band and eventually hired vocalist Frank Sinatra, resulting in a partnership that was instantly and mutually rewarding. Both Dorsey bands achieved years of musical and commercial success.

Glenn Miller formed his band in the late thirties, and by the early forties polls showed his to be the most popular dance band in the world. In 1942, at the height of his success, Miller joined the army, where

Count Basie
(1904–1984)

From inauspicious beginnings, first as a piano player in vaudeville, then in movie theaters, Count Basie joined Bennie Moten's band in the early 1930s. When Moten died in 1935, Basie took some of the musicians and formed his own band, which lasted until he was introduced to Benny Goodman by record producer John Hammond. He played in Goodman's band for a while, then went on to spend the next forty-five years either leading or playing in both large and small bands, with diverse personnel including musicians Buck Clayton, Lester Young, Dicky Wells, and Benny Morton; arrangers Eddie Durham, Jimmy Mundy, Don Redman, and Neal Hefti; and singers Helen Humes, Billie Holiday, Joe Williams, and Ella Fitzgerald. His popularity far outlasted the wane of the Big Band era, and the Count Basie Orchestra continues to play though Basie died in 1984.

he formed an all-star unit made up of other soldiers. The band played for U.S. troops, broadcasting over the Armed Forces Radio Network. Miller was on his way to France ahead of the band in 1944 when the small plane carrying him and two other passengers disappeared. The plane was never found.

Artie Shaw formed and reformed bands in the mid-thirties, trying to be unique. He achieved that goal in 1938 with the release of "Begin the Beguine," which, together with his skill on the clarinet, made him not only world famous, but a top contender for the "King of Swing" title. Shaw quit the business and left the country for Mexico at the height of his career in 1939, but, also in a familiar pattern, returned to the United States to form and reform bands throughout the forties.

Trumpeter Harry James made his record debut in Ben Pollack's band; he then played for Benny Goodman; finally, he formed his own band in 1939, achieving great success. James is credited with being the first to recognize the talents of a vocal-

Larry Clinton (1909–1985)

Although he began his career as a trumpet player, Larry Clinton became a superb arranger and composer, finally emerging as an example of an arranger with good business sense who could lead his own band. Beginning as an arranger for the Dorsey Brothers, Larry was left with Jimmy Dorsey when Tommy quit to form his own band. From there, Clinton went to Glen Gray and the Casa Loma Orchestra, and eventually to Tommy Dorsey, whose band he left to form his own in 1938. The height of his success was with vocalist Bea Wain, after which several vocalists came and went until Clinton, a pilot, joined the U.S. Air Force. After the war Larry went back to arranging and recording until he retired to Florida with his wife.

Red Nichols (1905–1965)

Cornet player Red Nichols and his band, which usually had only eight or nine and sometimes as few as five members, were already working steadily on the radio and in recording studios when the big band craze hit in the mid-thirties. Perhaps this is why he did not feel a need to record the commercial favorites of the time, but continued to play, with consistent excellence, his loose, jazzy numbers. Eventually both Dorsey brothers, Jack Teagarden, Gene Krupa, Glenn Miller, Benny Goodman, and many others would play with Nichols, who continued to lead his band through the forties. The sentimental 1959 Hollywood movie *The Five Pennies* brought a resurgence of success for him.

ist named Frank Sinatra, and the two remained friends long after Sinatra left to join Tommy Dorsey. In 1941, James added a

string quartet to his band and recorded "You Made Me Love You," which became an immediate hit. The Harry James band, like those of Benny Goodman, Woody Herman, Tommy Dorsey, and several others, disbanded in 1946.

By the early part of 1939, drummer Gene Krupa had left Benny Goodman to form his own band, which reached its height

Audiences and musicians alike thought Gene Krupa was America's greatest drummer.

with the additions of singer Anita O'Day and trumpeter Roy Eldridge. Drummer Buddy Rich, an extremely volatile performer, played with Tommy Dorsey, among others, before starting his own group in 1946, the same year so many other bands were shutting down.

Woody Herman

During his career, Woody Herman (1913–1987) was one of the most popular bandleaders, both with the public and musicians. As a leader, Woody made his sidemen feel they were playing with him, not for him. After his term with Isham Jones, the first band he formed was a cooperative that came to be known as "the band that plays the blues." They stuck to that theme but had little success until 1939, when their recording of "Wood-chopper's Ball" became a hit. The song, written by Joe Bishop, would be Woody's signature song for the rest of his long career.

Besides his easygoing personality, Woody Herman had other notable attributes. He was an excellent recruiter of talent; this, combined with his reputation as a great bandleader, made musicians eager

Red Norvo (b. 1908)

Xylophonist Red Norvo began his eight-man band in 1935. Formerly with the Paul Whiteman band, Norvo had learned how to make smooth, swinging sounds. However, this sound couldn't fill a large dance hall. Then, when powerful vocalist Mildred Bailey, who also happened to be Norvo's wife, and arranger Ed Sauter joined Red, Norvo's band was thought to really swing. He continued to lead the band with various members until the early forties, and thereafter worked with smaller instrumental groups.

Red Norvo and his band in action, 1938.

to work for him. When the war began, many musicians were drafted, and several orchestras were forced to disband, but Woody's reputation as a leader made it easier for him to replace his musicians. The band, called Herman's Herd, included pianist Ralph Burns (who came to him from Charlie Barnet's band), trumpeter/arranger Neal Hefti, drummer Dave Tough, bassist Chubby Jackson, and xylophonist Red Norvo.

Another of Woody's talents, for which he received high acclaim from critics and biographers (even though he never seemed to fully take advantage of it), was his singing ability. Many singers, mostly female, played short stints with Woody's band, but his is the voice heard on "Laura" and "Caldonia."

The Woody Herman Orchestra in 1946.

Trumpeter Dizzy Gillespie, a legendary jazz musician, performing in Carnegie Hall.

Always interested in diversity, Woody played the "Ebony" Concerto at Carnegie Hall in March 1946, written for him by his friend and fan Igor Stravinsky. Also in 1946, public polls declared Woody's band, now called the First Herd (which included a band-within-a-band called the Woodchoppers), the number one dance band. Along with this acclaim came abundant attention and advice from all quarters: business agents, record and radio producers, music promoters, and financial advisors. The flurry of activity began to cause discord within the band, and Woody, at the height of his popularity but ready for a rest, decided it was a good time to call it quits.

But inactivity did not suit him, and in 1947, Herman formed the Second Herd, which included Stan Getz and Zoot Sims. This band came to be known as the Four Brothers, after the success of the song with the same title, written by Jimmy Giuffre. Until his death in 1987, Woody Herman continued to re-form new bands, playing with talents such as Dizzy Gillespie, Rosemary Clooney, and Lionel Hampton.

Kay Kyser

Bandleaders came in all shapes and sizes and had assorted talents and personalities. Many, like Benny Goodman, Glenn Miller, Woody Herman, and the Dorsey Brothers, were musicians who became leaders. Singer Bob Crosby led his own band, called the Bob Cats. Still other musicians, such as Duke Ellington and Fletcher Henderson, were also writers and arrangers who formed their own organizations. Some, like Henderson, Louis Armstrong, Jimmie Lunceford, and Count Basie, created their own distinctive musical styles; others managed to effectively meld commercialism and innovative music, as did Glenn Miller and Tommy Dorsey. Trumpeter Clyde McCoy and His Orchestra became recognized for McCoy's distinctive "wah-wah" trumpet sound. Some bands, such as Guy Lombardo's and Lawrence Welk's, were thought by their peers to be of little musical merit, even though they were highly successful with the public.

And some people just wanted to lead a band. This is the category into which a trained lawyer who couldn't read or

Kay Kyser dresses for an appearance on the College of Musical Knowledge.

write a note of music named Kay Kyser (1906–1985) fit.

Although he wasn't a musician, Kay Kyser was a smart, shrewd, clever, and outgoing man. With his friend Johnny Mercer from the University of North Carolina, Kyser led many bands during the 1920s and early 1930s, with a style that ranged from sweet to jazz. In 1934, fellow alumnus Hal Kemp

Lawrence Welk (1903–1992)

Most of Lawrence Welk's peers had little regard for what they considered to be his middle-of-the-road music and his band's mediocre talent. But Welk, who spent his share of time on the road before his successful television dance show, had done his homework, and he delivered to the public exactly what it wanted: easy-to-listen-to, easy-to-dance-to, easy-to-forget-your-troubles-and-have-a-good-time-to orchestra music. His show, which originated in 1952 in the Aragon Ballroom in Santa Monica, California, was first shown on television in 1955 and exceeded all expectations for its commercial success.

suggested Kyser's band follow Kemp's at the popular Blackhawk Restaurant in Chicago, from which concerts were broadcast on the radio. Kyser's easy, pleasant style of music quickly endeared him to audiences, but the show was stopped by the actors' union, which had engineered a crackdown on programs that were not paying union scale. To get around the regulations, Kyser created a musical game involving amateur contestants

Bob Crosby (b. 1913)

Many of the musicians from Ben Pollack's band were disgruntled by what they thought was Pollack's lack of interest, and quit. In 1935, they reunited under Ben's former booker, Gil Rodin, who wanted to keep the band together but didn't want to be the bandleader. Francis O'Keefe of the Rockwell-O'Keefe agency provided Bob Crosby (brother of Bing) to act as leader. This arrangement worked well because Bob enjoyed his role but wasn't overbearing and allowed Gil Rodin to manage the band behind the scenes. The Bob Crosby Band played dixieland music, an unusual style for a big band, but they played it distinctively enough to please even New York audiences. When the band reformed after the end of the war, they caught the attention in Chicago of a wealthy widow named Mrs. Celeste LeBrosi, who became a patron, following them on tour and providing them with irresistible luxuries such as lavish parties and rented mansions for out-of-town engagements. The band eventually came to be called Bob Crosby and the Bob Cats, and enjoyed relatively uninterrupted success until the early 1940s.

from the Blackhawk's audience. Kyser dressed in a graduate's cap and gown, the band played a song, and the contestant had to guess the title. Thus began what is perhaps the forerunner of many game and quiz shows: Kay Kyser's *College of Musical Knowledge*. It became a huge success. Kyser sent bags of fan mail to the entertainment executives at MCA and convinced them that the show should be sold to a network.

As the band's leader, Kyser introduced some important innovations to radio, such as the "singing song title." Musicians would play the first line, and Kyser would introduce the song while the music continued. The result was to diminish "dead air" and save program time for more music. (This is a technique used in radio today; disc jockeys still talk over the opening bars of a piece of music.)

Kyser also included some novelty acts, such as the comedian Sully Mason and singer/trumpeter Merwyn Bogue, nicknamed "Ishkabibble." Kyser featured a wide range of vocalists, including Ginny Sims, Julie Conway, and one of America's favorites, Harry Babbitt, who sang "Jingle, Jangle, Jingle" with Conway.

He was funny and clever, but Kyser was not a frivolous man. During World War II, he tried unsuccessfully to enlist. Undaunted, he turned his talents to war service and refused to play engagements for anyone outside the armed forces. Kyser's career lasted through the forties, during which period the *College of Musical Knowledge* made it to TV. He retired to North Carolina, where he died in 1985.

Clyde McCoy (b. 1903)

Born in Kentucky, Clyde McCoy began playing trumpet on riverboats and at other local venues throughout the South; he formed his first band at age nineteen. In 1942, while still successful, he and his entire band joined the U.S. Navy. McCoy's rendition of the Clarence Williams song "Sugar Blues" has continued to be his trademark since he first recorded it in 1931.

Goodman's enormous success. Some of the most successful music arrangers evolved out of the orchestra, as did Ralph Burns and Neal Hefti. Others preferred to work on a freelance basis, as Eddie Sauter did for Artie Shaw, Benny Goodman, and Red Norvo. Henry Mancini, Nelson Riddle, Ray Conniff, and Johnny Mandel were all music arrangers.

On the business end of things, there were others equally responsible for the success of these bands, namely managers and bookers. Along with write-ups in trade magazines such as *Metronome* and *Down Beat*, the primary means of gaining exposure was through radio coverage and live performances. To get jobs, most bands relied on bookers, whose major interest was to find the most extensive possible exposure for the band, sometimes without regard for the physical challenge posed. Some bands had the luxury of a manager who did their booking, as Joe Glaser did for Louis

Other Key Members of a Big Band

Besides the bandleader, the person most responsible for creating a band's signature style was the arranger. Arrangers determined the specific musical part for each section, group, or soloist, and often played the role of coach to the musical team. Bandleaders Fletcher Henderson and Duke Ellington arranged most of their own music. After Henderson disbanded his orchestra, he became music arranger for Benny Goodman, contributing greatly to

Armstrong and others. In the early thirties, the management and booking office Rockwell-O'Keefe was formed; it was later renamed General Artists Corporation, or GAC. Eventually, Woody Herman, Glenn Miller, Tommy Dorsey, and Artie Shaw would all rely on GAC's management services. GAC's major competitor was Music Corporation of America (MCA), founded by Jules Stein and Billy Goodheart. Willard Alexander, who helped orchestrate Benny Goodman's first tour and also managed Count Basie, was an MCA agent until 1939, when he left to begin a band department at the William Morris agency.

The Movies

For anyone born later than the mid-forties, movies from the era are a good way to recapture the flavor of the big band experience. In some of these movies, where only a feeble effort was made to weave the band into the story, such as *Stage Door Canteen*, *Sweet and Low-Down*, and *Jam Session*, the music is the only remarkable element.

By late 1942, with the musicians' strike preventing recording sessions, and government gasoline and entertainment restrictions limiting attendance at live shows, Hollywood looked pretty attractive to bandleaders. And Hollywood producers were just beginning to grasp the commercial appeal of the bands. Woody Herman, Harry James, Tommy Dorsey, Jimmy Dorsey, Charlie Barnet, Glenn Miller, Benny Goodman, Artie Shaw, Bob Crosby, Gene Krupa, Stan Kenton, and Kay Kyser all eventually made their way to Hollywood. In an effort to conform to Hollywood conventions, musicians often looked out of place in the movies. Tommy Dorsey's *Las Vegas Night*, Gene Krupa's *Ball of Fire*, and Woody Herman's *Winter Wonderland* are all examples of movies that cast the musicians in patently unnatural situations.

There were a few commercial successes that were also fairly good movies, such as two with Glenn Miller, called *Sun Valley Serenade* and *Orchestra Wives*; The

Fleet's In, with Jimmy Dorsey's Band, featuring Bob Eberly and Helen O'Connell; and *Best Foot Forward*, with Harry James, who also starred in *Syncopation* with Benny Goodman.

Hollywood made many biographies of famous bandleaders that more often than not bore little resemblance to any real story. The most memorable of these were *The Benny Goodman Story*, starring Steve Allen; *The Gene Krupa Story*, with Sal Mineo; *The Glenn Miller Story*, with James Stewart as Miller and June Allyson as his wife; and *The Fabulous Dorseys*, starring Jimmy and Tommy themselves. In 1959, Danny Kaye played bandleader Red Nichols in a story about his life and his band called *The Five Pennies*, which featured great music by Nichols, Bob Crosby, and Louis Armstrong and brought a renewed vitality to Nichols' career.

Above: Sal Mineo played drummer Gene Krupa in The Gene Krupa Story. *Also in the cast, Giselle MacKenzie, Bobby Darin, and Jimmy Durante. Below: The cast of* Best Foot Forward *included Lucille Ball, far left, and Harry James, fifth from left.*

End of the Era

Conditions in the music industry worsened with the outbreak of World War II. For instance, in an effort to conserve gasoline, a 35-mile-per-hour speed limit was implemented, making it virtually impossible for a band to travel between cities for back-to-back, one-night engagements. In addition to gas rationing, the government also imposed a 20 percent amusement tax, making it too costly for most Americans to enjoy regular nights out.

World War II caused several changes within the structures of the bands. Many eligible musicians enlisted or were drafted, causing bandleaders to compete for good musicians to fill their vacant slots. By the time the United States became involved in the war, over 200 bands had signed up to entertain troops at USO functions and fund-raising rallies. Artie Shaw and Rudy Vallee, among others, joined Glenn Miller in enlisting in the service. Clyde McCoy was

Arranger and conductor Henry Mancini leads a recording session in 1964.

probably the first bandleader to join the service with his entire orchestra.

In the midst of these increasingly tough times, one more complication developed. James Caesar Petrillo, the newly elected president of the American Federation of Musicians, ordered his members to stop making records because radio stations and jukebox owners were not paying royalties.

The strike affected only instrumentalists—that is, all of the bands and orchestras. The curious part is that it did not affect singers. Many singers recorded a cappella.

Cab Calloway (b. 1907)

In the early 1920s, Cab Calloway began his career in St. Louis with Wilson Robinson's Syncopators. He then moved to New York's Cotton Club Orchestra (led at the time by violinist Andy Preer), which later came to be called the Missourians, with Calloway as its leader. Known for his superb voice, Calloway consistently thrilled audiences by singing ballads gracefully, although his preference was for singing popular novelty songs.

His band remained popular because of his choices of numbers, but also because he had very talented jazz musicians behind him, an uncharacteristic feature in many singer-led bands. Because of his faithful appreciation of good music, and because he paid well, his musicians were productive and loyal. When the Big Band era began to fizzle in the mid-forties, the popular and gregarious Calloway continued to lead smaller bands and to perform alone.

At a time when travel was reduced to a minimum and recording was reduced to nothing at all, this strike caused the popularity of big bands and dance music to suffer even more. When the war ended, the bans were lifted and the strike was ended—but a whole new genre of music, dominated by singers, had gained popularity. Big band music never again enjoyed its previous acclaim. But the unity, the precision, and the distinct personalities of each orchestra laid a solid foundation for much of the popular music (and a great deal of the jazz) of the future.

Listener's Guide

The following is a partial list of recordings selected because they are popular or superior examples of music from the big band era.

Duke Ellington

It Don't Mean a Thing If It Ain't Got That Swing (written by Duke Ellington, recorded 1932)

Take the A Train (arranged by Billy Strayhorn, recorded 1938)

Lazy Rhapsody (Duke Ellington, recorded 1932)

Mood Indigo (Duke Ellington, 1930)

St. Louis Blues (written by W.C. Handy, 1914; recorded 1932)

Creole Love Call (Duke Ellington, recorded 1932)

Caravan (Duke Ellington, 1937)

Blue Harlem (Duke Ellington, 1932)

Lightnin' (Duke Ellington, 1932)

Stormy Weather (written by Harold Arlen, recorded 1933)

Ain't Misbehavin' (written by Fats Waller, recorded 1933)

Moonglow (written by Will Hudson, 1934)

Showboat Shuffle (Duke Ellington, 1935)

Echoes of Harlem (Duke Ellington, 1935)

Don't Get Around Much Anymore (Duke Ellington, 1940)

When My Sugar Walks Down the Street (Duke Ellington, 1940)

I Got It Bad (and That Ain't Good) (Duke Ellington, 1941)

Satin Doll (Duke Ellington, 1938)

Bojangles (Duke Ellington, 1940)

Benny Goodman

King Porter Stomp (written by Jelly Roll Morton, 1924; arranged by Fletcher Henderson, 1935)

Blue Skies (written by Irving Berlin, 1927; arranged by Fletcher Henderson, 1935)

Between the Devil and the Deep Blue Sea (written by Harold Arlen, 1931)

Swingtime in the Rockies (arranged by Jimmy Mundy, 1936)

Jam Session (arranged by Jimmy Mundy, 1936)

If Dreams Came True (arranged by Edgar Sampson, 1938)

Don't Be That Way (arranged by Edgar Sampson, 1938)

Peckin' (written by Ben Pollack and Harry James, 1937)

Life Goes to a Party (arranged by Harry James, 1937)

Ridin' High (written by Cole Porter, arranged by Jimmy Mundy, 1936)

How High the Moon (arranged by Fletcher Henderson, 1939)

Cocoanut Grove (written by Harry Owens, 1938; arranged by Eddie Sauter, 1940)

My Old Flame (written by Arthur Johnston and Sam Coslow, 1934; arranged by Eddie Sauter, 1941)

Stompin' at the Savoy (written by Benny Goodman, 1936)

Louis Armstrong

I'm a Ding Dong Daddy (written by Phil Baxter, recorded 1929)

I Can't Give You Anything But Love (written by Jimmy McHugh, recorded 1929)

I Got Rhythm (written by George Gershwin, recorded 1930)

On The Sunny Side of the Street (written by Jimmy McHugh, 1930)

Georgia On My Mind (Hoagy Carmichael, recorded 1931)

Star Dust (written by Hoagy Carmichael, recorded 1931)

Swing That Music (written by Louis Armstrong, 1936)

Jubilee (written by Hoagy Carmichael and Stanley Adams, 1938)

Mahogany Hall Stomp (written by Spencer Williams, 1929)

When It's Sleepy Time Down South (written by Louis Armstrong, 1932)

Glenn Miller

I Got Rhythm (written by George Gershwin, 1937)

Moonlight Serenade (written by Glenn Miller, 1939)

In the Mood (written by Joe Garland, 1930; recorded 1939)

Sunrise Serenade (written by Frankie Carle, 1939)

Little Brown Jug (written by Joseph E. Winner, 1869; arranged by Bill Finegan, 1939)

Tuxedo Junction (written by Erskine Hawkins, recorded 1934)

Pennsylvania Six Five Thousand (arranged by Jerry Gray, 1940)

Lionel Hampton

Flying Home (written by Lionel Hampton and Benny Goodman, 1939)

Chop, Chop (arranged by Milt Buckner, 1944)

Blues in the News (arranged by Milt Buckner, 1942)

In the Bag (written by Robert Crowder, 1939)

Million Dollar Smile (arranged by Milt Buckner, 1944)

Hamp's Boogie Woogie (Lionel Hampton, 1940)

Salty Papa Blues (arranged by Milt Buckner, 1943)

Woody Herman

Woodsheddin' with Woody (written by Lowell Martin, 1941)

Hot Chestnuts (written by Robert Hartshell, 1941)

Northwest Passage (written by Woody Herman and Ralph Burns, 1945)

Fan It (Woody Herman and Ralph Burns, 1945)

Summer Sequence (Woody Herman and Ralph Burns, 1946)

Ebony Concerto (written by Igor Stravinsky, 1946)

Count Basie

Jumpin' at the Woodside (written by Count Basie, 1938)

Oh, Lady Be Good (written by George Gershwin, 1936)

One O'Clock Jump (written by Count Basie, 1937)

My Heart Belongs To Daddy (written by Cole Porter, 1937)

Clap Hands, Here Comes Charlie (written by Joseph Meyer, 1925; arranged by Jimmy Mundy, 1939)

Lester Leaps In (written by Lester Young, 1939)

Tommy Dorsey

I'm Getting Sentimental Over You (written by George Bassman and Ned Washington, 1932)

Tea For Two (written by Vincent Youmans, 1924; arranged by Sy Oliver, 1939)

Blue Moon (written by Richard Rodgers and Lorenz Hart, 1934; arranged by Sy Oliver, 1939)

I Get A Kick Out Of You (written by Cole Porter, 1934, recorded 1939)

Jimmie Lunceford

White Heat (written by Will Hudson, 1934)

Jazznocracy (written by Will Hudson, 1934)

Stratosphere (written by Jimmie Lunceford, 1934)

Stomp It Off (arranged by Sy Oliver 1934)

Lunceford Special (written by Snooky Young, 1939)

Jimmy Dorsey

Don't Be That Way (written by Mitchell Parish, Benny Goodman, Edgar Sampson, 1938)

Tangerine (written by Johnny Mercer and Victor Schertzinger, 1942)

In a Sentimental Mood (written by Duke Ellington, 1935, arranged by Bobby Byrne, 1936)

Major and Minor Stomp (arranged by Joe Lippman, 1939)

Recommended Reading

Berendt, Joachim E. *The Jazz Book: From Ragtime to Fusion and Beyond.* Westport, Connecticut: Lawrence Hill & Co., 1975.

Feather, Leonard. *The Encyclopedia of Jazz.* New York: Da Capo Press, 1960.

Gleason, Ralph J. *Jam Session.* New York: Putnam's, 1958.

Hentoff, Nat and Albert J. McCarthy. *Jazz.* New York: Da Capo Press, 1975.

Keepnews, Orrin, and Bill Grauer. *A Pictorial History of Jazz.* New York: Crown, 1955.

Kinkle, Roger D. *The Complete Encyclopedia of Popular Music and Jazz 1900-1950,* Vols. 1-4. Westport, Connecticut: Arlington House Publishers, 1974.

Shapiro, Nat and Nat Hentoff. *Hear Me Talkin' To Ya.* New York: Dover Publications, 1966.

Index